BACKYARD
SCIENTIST

BACKYARD
CHEMISTRY
EXPERIMENTS

Alix Wood

PowerKiDS
press

New York

Published in 2019 by Rosen Publishing
29 East 21st Street, New York, NY 10010

Produced for Rosen Publishing by Alix Wood Books
Designed by Alix Wood
Editor: Eloise Macgregor
Projects devised and photographed by Kevin Wood

Photo credits:
Cover, 1, 4, 5, 6 top, 25 bottom © Adobe Stock Images;
all other photos © Kevin Wood

Cataloging-in-Publication Data
Names: Wood, Alix.
Title: Backyard chemistry experiments / Alix Wood.
Description: New York : PowerKids Press, 2019. | Series: Backyard scientist | Includes glossary
and index.
Identifiers: LCCN ISBN 9781538337387 (pbk.) | ISBN 9781538337370 (library bound) |
ISBN 9781538337394 (6 pack)
Subjects: LCSH: Chemistry--Experiments--Juvenile literature.
Classification: LCC QD43.W64 2019 | DDC 540.78--dc23

Printed in the United States of America

CPSIA compliance information: Batch # CS18PK: For further information contact Rosen Publishing, New York, New York at 1-800-237-9932.

Contents

What Is Chemistry?

Chemistry is the study of the materials that everything is made from. Chemists study what different **substances** can do, what they are made of, and if and how they might change. Knowing all about chemistry is very useful. Doctors use chemistry to develop medicine. Farmers use it to help crops grow. Chefs use chemistry to create great food. Chemistry is also fun! Try the experiments in this book and find out about chemistry for yourself.

Detective Work

To find out exactly what a mystery substance is, chemists do tests and ask questions. They might try to find out what temperature a liquid boils or freezes at, or see if a substance dissolves in water. Chemists might test to see if a substance is just one thing, or a mixture of things. Maybe they want to find out if it changes when it is heated, or if it changes back when it is cooled again.

Setting Up Your Backyard Laboratory

Find an outside space that you can use to do these experiments. Some of them are pretty messy! Remember to check with whomever owns the space that it is OK to do your experiments there. You may want to find a picnic table to work on.

You should be able to find most of the things you will need around your home or yard. You may need to buy some small items, so check the "You Will Need" section before you start a project.

BE SCIENTIFIC

Be a scientist. Think of an idea that you want to prove or **disprove**. Then do an experiment to test the idea.

To create a fair test, try to just change one thing at a time. Repeat your experiment to check your result wasn't a **fluke**. Take notes. Was your idea correct? Can you draw a conclusion?

STAYING SAFE

Science experiments can be dangerous. The experiments in this book have been specially chosen because they are fun and relatively safe, but you must still be careful. Ask an adult to help you. Follow all warnings. Wear any suggested protective clothing, and be careful.

Minty Geysers

What happens when you add a packet of mints to a bottle of cola? It gets messy! Make sure you try this experiment in a big, open space. The experiment works best with diet cola, as it has slightly different ingredients from regular cola. Make sure the cola is not past its sell-by date, too.

1

Roll some paper tightly around the packet of mints. Cut away any excess paper. Secure the cylinder using a small piece of tape.

2

Check that the cylinder fits inside the top of the bottle. It needs to be able to easily slide in and out.

3

Unwrap the mints. Place them in the cylinder. Hold a hand over the bottom of the cylinder to keep the mints from falling out.

4

Place the bottle in an open space. Stand well back. Ask an adult to unscrew the lid and quickly push the mints through the cylinder into the bottle. Then run!

5

WHAT'S HAPPENING?

Soda has **carbon dioxide** gas in it. It is the carbon dioxide which makes it fizz. When you drop the Mentos into the bottle, tiny bubbles form around each of the small dents on the sugar coating. As the mints sink, the gas bubbles push the soda up with an incredible force!

Ice Cube Fishing

Did you know that water can be a solid, a liquid, or a gas? Water becomes a solid when it is frozen, and a gas when it is heated. A **solution** of water mixed with dissolved salt has a lower **freezing point** than pure water. Use this science fact to go ice cube fishing!

YOU WILL NEED:

- bowl of cold water
- ice cube tray
- colored construction paper
- scissors
- table salt
- a piece of string

1

Draw some small fish shapes on the construction paper. They need to be small enough to fit in an ice cube. Cut them out.

2

Half-fill an ice cube tray with water. Place a fish in each cube, and then fill to the top with more water. Put the tray in the freezer and wait until the cubes have frozen.

3

Pour some cold water in a bowl. Put the fishy ice cubes in the water.

4

Lay some string over the ice cubes. Lift the string and see if you can lift any fish out of the bowl. Did you catch any?

5

Sprinkle a pinch of salt on the water. Lay the string over the ice cubes and wait a few moments. Gently lift the string. Did you catch any fish this time?

WHAT'S HAPPENING?

When salt is sprinkled on ice, the ice melts. With just a small amount of salt, the water around the ice cubes quickly freezes again. The string gets trapped in the refreezing water, making it stick to the ice cube.

The Exploding Bag

The ice experiment showed some changes can be reversible. That is, the melted ice can be changed back to how it was before. Most **chemical reactions** are **irreversible**, and cannot be changed back. Watch this amazing chemical reaction that makes a bag explode before your eyes!

1 Take a square piece of paper towel. Place 1 1/2 tablespoons of baking soda onto the center of your paper towel square.

2 Fold your paper towel up with the baking soda inside. Then leave it to one side.

3

Place 1/2 cup of water and 1/4 cup of vinegar into the ziplock bag. You can add food coloring.

4

Outside, quickly drop the baking soda parcel into the bag and seal it shut. Shake the bag, then put it down and walk a small distance away. Then watch what happens.

5

The bag will start to fill up with carbon dioxide gas. After a few seconds your bag should explode!

WHAT'S HAPPENING?

Mixing baking soda and vinegar together creates a chemical reaction. The ingredients react to make carbon dioxide gas. The reaction produces so much gas that it fills the bag and then runs out of room, causing the bag to explode!

Giant Bubbles

It's fun to make your own enormous bubbles. First, pick the right weather conditions. Sunshine and wind may dry out your bubbles and make them pop. An overcast day with no wind is best. If the weather is sunny, you could take your bubbles to a shady area and use them there. Try this great bubble recipe.

YOU WILL NEED:

- 6 cups of water
- 1/2 cup dish soap, such as Dawn (not antibacterial)
- 1/2 cup cornstarch
- 1 tbsp baking powder
- 1 tbsp glycerin
- a spoon

1 Put the water in a bowl. **Distilled water** works best. Add the cornstarch. Mix with a spoon until all the cornstarch dissolves.

2 Stir in the remaining ingredients. Mix carefully so you do not create a froth.

MAKE A GIANT BUBBLE WAND

You can make a giant bubble wand like the one below out of a piece of cable. Just form it into a circle and twist the bottom to make a handle. You could also bend a wire coat hanger into a circle and wrap yarn around it. The yarn helps the mixture stick to the wand.

Let the mixture rest for an hour. Stir occasionally as the cornstarch settles to the bottom. Don't worry if some cornstarch won't dissolve.

WHAT'S HAPPENING?

Bubbles form when the **atoms** that make up water attract each other and create **surface tension**. The soap helps the water stretch and make a sphere shape. The glycerin makes the bubbles last longer, by slowing down the **evaporation** of the water.

Soap-Powered Boat

Water **molecules** are attracted to each other. Their attraction creates a flexible skin on the surface, known as surface tension. Surface tension helps objects float on water. See what happens if you remove the surface tension from one side of a floating object using dish soap.

YOU WILL NEED:

- large basin or bowl
- thin paper or tracing paper
- construction paper
- scissors
- liquid soap, such as Dawn

1

Trace around the template on page 15. Cut a few boat shapes from the construction paper, using your template.

2

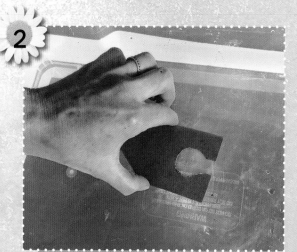

Fill the basin with water. Place the boat gently so it is flat on the surface of the water. It should float.

3

Put a drop of the dish soap behind the boat.

Your boat should quickly move forward!

4

boat template

WHAT'S HAPPENING?

Surface tension holds your boat on the surface. As the surface tension is the same on all sides, your boat doesn't move. Adding soap lowers the surface tension behind the boat. The boat is then pulled forward by the stronger surface tension in front of the boat.

15

Growing Crystals

Crystals are beautiful natural structures that form a repeating pattern. Diamonds and snowflakes are both types of crystal. Crystals form when liquids cool and start to harden, or when water evaporates. Salt crystals form when salt water evaporates. Try growing your own crystals with this experiment.

1

Place the pan on the black paper. Draw around the bottom of the pan. Cut out the circle, just inside the outline you drew. Then put the circle in the bottom of the pan.

2

Stir 1 tablespoon of Epsom salt into 1/4 cup of warm water. Stir until the salt is dissolved.

3

Pour the solution into the cake pan.

4

Put the pan in the sunshine. As the water evaporates, you'll see needle-like crystals start to form.

5

To clearly see their amazing shapes, look at your crystals through a magnifying glass.

WHAT'S HAPPENING?

Epsom salt is another name for magnesium sulfate. As the salt solution evaporates, the magnesium sulfate atoms run into each other. When the atoms join together, they form a crystal structure.

Watercolor Ice Melts

Solutions don't all freeze at the same temperature. They have different freezing points, the temperature they need to reach before they start to freeze. Salt melts ice because it lowers water's freezing point. Can you predict which type of salt will melt the ice the fastest?

YOU WILL NEED:

- bowls for making the ice
- large tray with sides
- table salt, rock salt, sea salt
- food coloring
- droppers or a spoon

1 Fill a few bowls with water and freeze them overnight. Meanwhile, collect different types of salt, and food coloring.

2 Loosen the ice from the bowls by holding them under warm running water. Place the ice blocks onto the tray.

3

Sprinkle a different type of salt over each ice block. The ice should start to melt. Which one melts the ice the quickest?

WHAT'S HAPPENING?

All the salts speed up the melting process. Usually, table salt will melt ice more quickly, as the grains are smaller and cover the ice better.

4

Using a spoon or dropper, drop some food coloring over the ice blocks. The colors help show up the shapes that form, as the salt melts the ice.

Your ice will look amazing if you hold it up so the sun shines through it.

Make Your Own Bricks

People have been building using mud bricks for thousands of years. Clay soil is mixed with straw, leaves, or even animal dung. Once they are baked, or left in the sun to dry, the bricks become strong, fireproof, and waterproof. You can build all kinds of things using mud bricks.

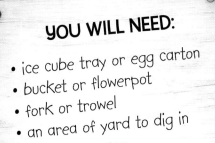

YOU WILL NEED:

- ice cube tray or egg carton
- bucket or flowerpot
- fork or trowel
- an area of yard to dig in
- straw or grass
- water

1 Ask an adult for permission to dig a hole in your yard. Using the fork or trowel, dig down until you reach heavy soil, usually found under the darker topsoil.

2 Collect enough soil to fill the ice cube tray or egg carton. Add a handful of straw or grass.

3

Gradually mix in a little water, until it is a thick mud.

4

Press the mud into your container. Get rid of any air bubbles by banging the container on the ground several times.

5

Let the bricks dry for a few days in a sunny place. Take them out of the container to dry for a few hours. Then build something amazing!

WHAT'S HAPPENING?

Mud is not as strong as mud mixed with straw. Many things are made from **composite material**—that is, two or more materials that, when combined, make **another useful material.**

Chalk Rockets

These exploding chalk rockets are fun, but be careful. If you use a canister that doesn't have a hinged lid, place it lid-side down once you've put the antacid tablet in. If a canister doesn't explode, wait a minute before checking it. It could go off in your face. After waiting, an adult can carefully check if the lid is on tight. If some of the gas leaks out slowly it won't work.

1

Mix 1 cup of water and 1 cup of cornstarch in a bowl. This will give you your base sidewalk chalk.

2

Pour the chalk mixture into the canisters or candy tubes until they are around 1/3 full.

3

Add a few drops of food coloring and mix well.

4

Break the antacid tablet in half. Put both pieces into a canister and quickly close the lid. Stand back!

The canister will jump in the air and explode the sidewalk paint. You could put some paper under your rockets to make some cool chalk art!

WHAT'S HAPPENING?

Dropping the antacid tablet into the mixture creates carbon dioxide gas. The gas creates a buildup of pressure inside the canister, which eventually pops the cap off and launches the canister into the air.

23

Try Walking on Water!

Usually, substances change their state from solid to liquid to gas when we change their temperature, such as water freezing into ice. Oobleck changes state when there are changes in pressure, instead. It can be both a solid and a liquid at the same time!

1

Pour a cup of cornstarch into a mixing bowl. Feel the powder in your hands. It is made up of very fine **particles**.

2

Slowly mix in a cup of water, until it is a thick mixture that hardens if you tap it. Add cornstarch if it is too runny, and water if it is too solid.

3

Slap your hand quickly onto the oobleck. It will seem solid.

WHAT'S HAPPENING?

Applying pressure to oobleck makes it feel hard because it forces the tiny cornstarch particles together. A gentle movement gives the cornstarch particles time to move away.

4

Slowly lower your hand into the oobleck. It will seem like liquid.

If you have a small kiddie pool and plenty of cornstarch, try this! Mix equal amounts of cornstarch and water to make a layer of oobleck on the bottom of your pool. Can you walk across without sinking?

Oobleck will clog your drains. Bag it and put it in the trash.

Make a Bouncy Ball

Did you know you can make your own bouncy ball? Try this fun experiment, but a word of caution — borax can irritate some people's skin. Make sure to wear rubber or latex gloves when you are making and playing with the bouncy ball. If you think you may be allergic to borax or starch or latex gloves, don't do this project!

YOU WILL NEED:

- 1 tbsp borax or laundry starch
- 1/2 cup warm water
- 2 tbsp PVA glue
- 1 tbsp cornstarch
- food coloring and glitter (optional)
- 2 mixing bowls
- rubber or latex gloves

ADULT HELP NEEDED

1

Mix the laundry starch or borax with the warm water in a bowl. Stir until the powder is dissolved.

2

In another mixing bowl, mix together the cornstarch and glue. You can add food coloring or glitter, too.

3

Add 1/2 teaspoon of the borax mixture to the glue and cornstarch mixture. Wait 15 seconds.

4

Add the rest of the borax mix. Start to form it into a ball. The more you work it, the firmer the ball will get.

WHAT'S HAPPENING?

A chemical reaction takes place between the borax or laundry starch and the glue, creating chains of molecules. The cornstarch helps bind the molecules together.

Are you a chemistry genius? Test yourself with these questions. The answers are on page 29.

1. Which of these statements is true?
a) Chemistry is the study of the weather
b) Chemistry is the study of substances
c) Chemistry is the study of animals

2. To create a fair scientific test, what should you do?
a) change just one thing in your test each time
b) change everything in your test each time

3. What helps an object float on water?
a) if the object is heavy
b) putting blue dye in the water
c) surface tension

4. What are the three states of matter?
a) solid, liquid, and gas
b) ice, water, and steam

5. Which of these is a crystal?
a) a potato   b) a diamond   c) water

6. What effect does salt have on ice?

a) it lowers the freezing point and causes it to melt

b) it makes the freezing point higher and causes it to freeze more

7. Which of these chemical reactions is reversible, so you can change the substances back to how they were again?

a) mixing baking soda and vinegar

b) melting an ice cube

c) making scrambled egg

8. What effect does the carbon dioxide have in a bottle of soda?

a) it makes it go flat

b) it makes it taste nice

c) it makes it fizzy

9. Every substance freezes at the same temperature.

a) true   b) false

10. Carbon dioxide is

a) a gas   b) a liquid   c) a solid

Glossary

atoms The smallest particle of an element.

carbon dioxide A heavy, colorless gas.

chemical reactions A process in which atoms of the same or different elements rearrange themselves to form a new substance.

composite material Two or more different materials combined together to create a superior and unique material.

disprove To prove to be false.

distilled water Water that has been made purer by being heated until it becomes a gas and then cooled.

evaporation The process of becoming vapor from a liquid state.

fluke Something that happens by accident or because of luck.

freezing point The temperature at which a liquid turns into a solid when cooled.

irreversible Impossible to reverse.

molecules The smallest particle of a substance.

particles Very small parts of matter (such as molecules, atoms, or electrons).

solution A liquid in which something has been dissolved.

substances The physical materials from which something is made.

surface tension The property of a liquid surface displayed by its acting as if it were a stretched elastic membrane.

For More Information

Amson-Bradshaw, Georgia. *Materials.* London, UK: Wayland, 2018.

Chatterton, Crystal. *Awesome Science Experiments for Kids: 100+ Fun STEAM Projects and Why They Work.* Emeryville, CA: Rockridge Press, 2018.

Ives, Rob. *Fun Experiments with Matter: Invisible Ink, Giant Bubbles, and More.* Minneapolis, MN: Hungry Tomato, 2017.

Slingerland, Janet. *Explore Atoms and Molecules!* White River Junction, VT: Nomad Press, 2017.

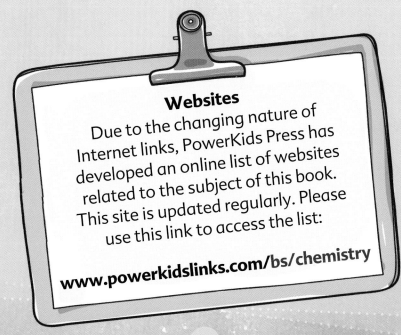

Websites

Due to the changing nature of Internet links, PowerKids Press has developed an online list of websites related to the subject of this book. This site is updated regularly. Please use this link to access the list:

www.powerkidslinks.com/bs/chemistry